FOREWARD

"I'm Growing Places" is the wonderful and inspiring story of a 6-year old farmer planting a seed in her patio garden in Atlanta, Georgia and taking us on the exciting journey to its harvest. The beauty of *"I'm Growing Places"* lies in its ability to educate readers about the basic tenets of agriculture in a fun and engaging way. As you turn each page you realize this book has the power to instill pride in young people from any background to farm while it creates the passion to grow food anywhere! The story is as inspiring, as is the journey of Kendall Rae Johnson, Georgia's youngest certified farmer and 4-H leader. The seeds Kendall Rae's grandmother planted in her, watered and nurtured by her loving parents, demonstrates how belief, education and the support of a loving family instill seeds for success. In *"I'm Growing Places"* the story ends with a beautiful garden. As for Kendall Rae, her full beauty, promising future and impact have yet to be seen! I encourage everyone to open the cover of *"I'm Growing Places"* and enjoy the fun journey of a seed all the way to Kendall Rae's harvest for her own table.

By Dr. Jewel Bronaugh,
Former United States Department of Agriculture,
Deputy Secretary

I'M GROWING PLACES

FOR THE KENDALL RAE JOHNSON'S OF THE WORLD WHO LIKE TO EXPLORE AND PLAY IN THE MUD. GETTING YOUR HANDS DIRTY, AINT NEVER HURT NO BODY!. THIS BOOK IS DEDICATED TO YOU ALL.

–U.K.J AND Q.E.J

The artist used markers on paper to create the illustration, then transferred to photoshop for this book.

EPUB Edition © 2022
ISBN: 9798887221458

10 9 8 7 6 5 4 3 2 1

First Edition

Contributors: Kendall Rae Johnson, Quentin Johnson, Ursula Kendall-Johnson and John E. Doyle

Illustrator: Brian Hebert

THANK YOU, THANK YOU, THANK YOU, THANK YOU!

THIS BOOK BELONGS TO A FUTURE GROWER!

_____

_____

WHAT IS YOUR NAME?

_____

_____

WHAT WOULD YOU LIKE TO GROW?

_____

_____

I'm Growing Places and so can you.

You can grow on a patio, that's where I started too.

Tomatoes, Peppers, Cucumbers that's what I grew.

The seed was so small it was hard
to see.

I put it in the ground because that is
where it grows.

But there is more to do and now
I know.

You have to water it and let the sun shine too.

Nature is smart she knows what to do.

One morning I woke up with an excited feeling.

I went to my garden a saw a baby seedling.

I shouted "I see it, it's starting to grow".

Now the next step what will this seedling show.

The next week there was a gentle summer breeze.

And now in my garden my seedling had sprouted leaves I'm seeing how things grow I am starting to understand It's now turned into a plant after being planted in the land.

I wondered what will be the next
adventure I will encounter
The next day.

I found out when the plant turned
into a flower!

But, it's not done, it's not over.

Now my flower turned into
a cucumber.

Now it's time to cut it from the vine.

To see it grow it has taken some time.

Seeing this process has been so neat.

Now I have my very own vegetable
to eat.

I love growing fruits and vegetables
yes I do.

And I hope after reading my story
so will YOU!

KENDALL RAE JOHNSON'S STORY

FACEBOOK @AGROWKULTURE
INSTAGRAM @AGROWKULTURE
TWITTER @GROWKULTURE
TIKTOK @AGROWKULTURE

KENDALL RAE JOHNSON, GEORGIA'S YOUNGEST CERTIFIED FARMER AT AGE OF 6, BORN AND RAISED IN ATLANTA, GEORGIA. KENDALL RAE, AS SHE IS KNOWN BY MOST, HAS BEEN PLAYING IN THE SOIL SINCE SHE WAS 3 YEARS OLD. SHE WAS INSPIRED BY THE TEACHINGS OF HER GREAT GRANDMOTHER LAURA "KATE" WILLIAMS. ALTHOUGH KENDALL RAE DOESN'T QUITE REMEMBER HER GREAT-GRAND, SHE REMEMBERS HEARING HER SAYING, "DON'T THROW MY COLLARD GREEN STEMS AWAY, PUT THEM BACK IN THE DIRT." THAT'S WHEN IT ALL STARTED...ON A SMALL, BUT MIGHTY LITTLE PATIO PORCH WITH GREAT GRANDMA. THIS TRANQUIL AND COMFORTING PLACE WAS WHERE THEY PLANTED SEEDS OF CUCUMBERS, PEPPERS, TOMATOES AND BROKEN COLLARD GREEN STEMS. KENDALL WAS FASCINATED BY WHAT WAS ONCE TINY SEEDS OR STEMS NOW HAD GROWN INTO A BEAUTIFUL GARDEN WITH COLORFUL VEGETABLES READY TO BE EATEN BY THE FAMILY.

TODAY, THIS 7 YEAR OLD IS THE YOUNGEST CERTIFIED FARMER IN THE STATE OF GEORGIA AND YOUNGEST REGISTERED WORLDWIDE WITH A PROFIT BUSINESS, NAMED AGROWKULTURE URBAN FARM. KENDALL HAS NOW A NON-PROFIT FOR AGRICULTURE EDUCATION, RESEARCH AND YOUTH DEVELOPMENT, NAMED KENDALL RAE'S GREEN HEART. SHE HAS OBTAINED HER FARM AND TRACT ID, WITH THE FSA, OF USDA. KENDALL RAE'S LOVE OF FARMING AND SIMPLY GROWING HAS EMPOWERED HER TO BECOME AN ADVOCATE AND SPOKESPERSON FOR LITTLE PEOPLE ACROSS THE STATE OF GEORGIA AND BEYOND.

THERE'S NO DOUBT, THAT KENDALL RAE IS CREATING A MOVEMENT FOR YOUTH TODAY AND THE FUTURE. JOIN KENDALL RAE JOHNSON AND HER FRIENDS IN BECOMING CONSERVATION AND SOIL AMBASSADORS.

I'M GROWING PLACES

HI!, NEW AGROWKULTURIST, SOIL SCIENTIST AND CONSERVATIONIST. I'M SO EXCITED YOU ARE GROWING WITH ME. LETS CONTINUE TO GROW.

READ ME YOUR FAVORITS LINE FROM THE BOOK, "I'M GROWING PLACES" AND TAG ME ON SOCIAL MEDIA SO MY FRIENDS AND I CAN CONNECT WITH YOU AND SEND YOU SOME OF OUR FAVORITE THINGS TO DO ON THE FARM.

HINT: WE LIKE TO COLOR OUR VEGGIES AND FRUIT.

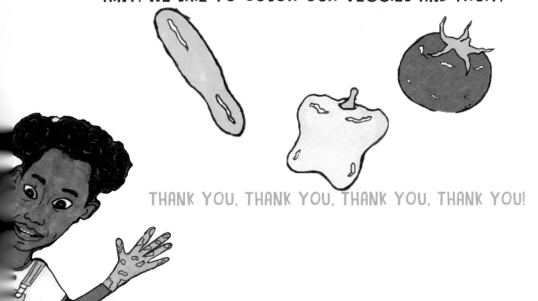

THANK YOU, THANK YOU, THANK YOU, THANK YOU!

Made in the USA
Columbia, SC
06 April 2024

33870453R00015